guys, let's keep it REAL!

Also from the Boys Town Press

Who's Raising Your Child?
Common Sense Parenting®
Fathers, Come Home
Parenting to Build Character in Your Teen
Common Sense Parenting of Toddlers and Preschoolers
Common Sense Parenting Learn-at-Home Video or DVD Kit
Angry Kids, Frustrated Parents
Dealing with Your Kids' 7 Biggest Troubles
Parents and Kids Talking About School Violence
Practical Tools for Foster Parents
Safe and Effective Secondary Schools
Teaching Social Skills to Youth
Tools for Teaching Social Skills in School
The Well-Managed Classroom
Unmasking Sexual Con Games
The Ongoing Journey
Journey of Faith
Journey of Hope
Journey of Love

For Adolescents

Little Sisters, Listen Up!
Boundaries: A Guide for Teens
A Good Friend
Who's in the Mirror?
What's Right for Me?

For a free Boys Town Press catalog, call 1-800-282-6657
Visit our web site at www.boystownpress.org

A Message of Hope
for Boys Growing Up in Poverty, Racism, and Despair

by
Farrell Artis

BOYS TOWN, NEBRASKA

Guys, Let's Keep It Real!
Published by the Boys Town Press
Father Flanagan's Boys' Home
Boys Town, NE 68010

Copyright © 2005, by Father Flanagan's Boys' Home

ISBN 1-889322-66-0

The Boys Town Press is the publishing division
of Girls and Boys Town, the original Father
Flanagan's Boys' Home.

Publishers' Cataloging-in-Publication Data

Artis, Farrell.

    Guys, let's keep it real! : a message of hope to boys growing up in
    poverty, racism, and despair / by Farrell Artis. -- 1st ed. -- Boys Town,
    NE : Boys Town Press, 2005.

        p. ; cm.

        ISBN: 1-889322-66-0

        1.†Social work with teenagers. 2.†Social work with youth.
    3.†Teenage boys. 4.†Poor teenagers. 5.†Child welfare. I.†Title.

HV1423 .A78 2005

362.7/083--dc22   0504

10   9   8   7   6   5   4   3   2   1

Table of Contents

"The ultimate measure
of a man is not where
he stands in moments of
comfort and convenience,
but where he stands at
times of challenge and
controversy."

——————————— **Martin Luther King, Jr.**
Clergyman and Civil Rights Leader
(1928 - 1968)

This African American man was born in Atlanta,
Georgia, the son of a pastor. As a child, King loved
books and was a gifted speaker. King worked hard
in school and was an excellent student. He chose
to become a minister and went on to college. He
continued his studies and received a master's and
doctorate degree. In the 1950s, Dr. King became

involved in the civil rights movement, and eventually became its most prominent leader. He believed that nonviolence and peaceful tactics were the best way to solve racial inequalities. In 1964, Dr. King was awarded the Nobel Peace Prize, becoming the youngest recipient of that honor in history. In 1968, Dr. King was assassinated while attempting to help others. The U.S. Congress voted to observe a national holiday in his honor, beginning in 1986, on the third Monday in January. Dr. King's hope and vision of equality for all and his message of love and peace continue to inspire many African Americans to work for nonviolent solutions to racial injustices.

Two Paths, Two Destinations

Farrell

"Hi, guys. My name is Farrell. I want to share with you some important things I learned growing up, so let's talk for a bit. First, let me tell you a little about myself. I'm a lot more like you than you might think.

"I was raised in Silsbee, Texas. It's a town located just outside of Houston. I grew up in what we called a 'shotgun' house. It was real long but not very wide. There was one main floor that had three bedrooms for me, my mom and dad, and my two sisters and four brothers. There were rows and rows of houses just like mine that went on for blocks. My mom and dad made sure we kept the house clean and the yard in good shape. Other people in the neighborhood didn't seem to care. They let their yards wither away and become overgrown with weeds and littered with junk. Some houses were rundown and badly in need of repairs.

"Growing up in my community, I remember being scared, even during the daytime. It was common to see arguments – even those between family members and friends – turn violent and end up being settled with fists, knives, and, oftentimes, guns. I knew people who were shot and killed or who shot and killed others. I even experienced this in my own family. Alcohol, drugs, and sex were there for the taking. People drove their cars through the neighborhoods blasting loud music from their stereos. Tension constantly hung in the air because we never knew when someone was going to get beat down or cut with a knife or shot and killed. Lots of times I wondered if it would to happen to me.

"There were certain streets and blocks that I didn't go near unless I had to. Just three blocks from my house was Pine Street, where there was a place called the Keystone Club. This was a club where danger lurked. Inside and outside the building, people drank, did drugs, and fought. I remember thinking there was a whole other world inside that club.

"I had to go by the Keystone Club to get to the

grocery store. When I went, I always rode my bike with a group of kids. Actually, I didn't do much alone. It was safer to be with a group. When we'd pass by the Keystone Club, the people hanging around outside would try to scare us or tell us what to do in life while they had a 40-ounce in one hand and drugs in the other.

"I was one of the lucky few in my community whose parents were married and lived under the same roof. Most of my friends lived with their moms; their fathers lived in the neighborhood but didn't stay at the same home. Many families lived off welfare. My dad provided for us. He worked 12-hour days as a welder. My mom took good care of us. I remember having to be home for dinner every night to eat with my family. My mom even cleaned other people's homes to help bring in extra money. My brothers, sisters, and I were expected to make our beds and do other chores around the house before we could go play with friends. And my parents made sure we were all getting our homework done.

"I enjoyed school. My older brother was a very good student. He always encouraged me to focus on my studies. I worked hard to get my homework done and get good grades. From middle school through high school, I was always involved in some kind of extracurricular activity: writing for the school newspaper and yearbook, writing and reading poetry, participating in spelling bees, and many other academic kinds of activities. I was one of the few African American students to participate in these kinds of things. Also, I played basketball. As a freshman in high school, I made the varsity. I was a good player and we had excellent teams all four years I played.

"I had the opportunity to travel a lot throughout Texas participating in school competitions and basketball games. These were wonderful experiences for me and they probably saved my life. I was able to get outside my community and see and meet people from other cultures. I was able to see with my own eyes and ears new places and new people and form my own opinion about others who were different from me.

"After high school, I went to a junior college in Texas where I played basketball and studied to become a teacher and coach. After two years, I moved on to a college in Missouri and played some ball and continued to study hard. During my college years, I made some poor choices. It was tough being away from my home and family. But I never gave up.

"I graduated from college, and today have a great job at Girls and Boys Town, where I help troubled kids and families. I'm married to a wonderful woman and have four fantastic kids. Also, I'm very active in the community helping others. I've got a great life. I made it out, and I want to do everything I can to help others make it out and succeed. And that includes you!

Terrance

"When I was growing up, Terrance was 'the man.' He was two years older than me, but he always treated me great. Terrance lived with his mother, sister, and brother. His mom was a good mother and she provided a good home.

"Terrance had everything going for him. He was popular and he did well in school when he tried. But what Terrance was most gifted at was sports. He was a natural athlete who was unusually big, strong, and fast for his age. In high school, Terrance was the star quarterback on the varsity football team. As a junior, Division I colleges were already recruiting him to play football for their schools. Terrance had a bright future and a great chance to make it out and be successful.

"But even when he first got to high school, Terrance started making bad choices. He was always joking and playing around, and he didn't take his schoolwork seriously. It didn't take long before Terrance was involved in drinking, drugs, and sex. Teachers and coaches looked the other way because Terrance was such a great athlete. He got a free ride in school, and people in the community gave him whatever he wanted, including alcohol and drugs. Even though he was messed up the night before, Terrance was always able to be a star on the football field. And that's all that mattered to most people.

"One day, in Terrance's junior year of high school, the community was having a softball tournament and a concert afterwards. It seemed like everyone was out and about having a good time. Terrance was with a big group of people. He was holding court, talking about sports. An older guy, Dwight, came up and wanted to talk about cars. Soon, the two were arguing back and forth, threatening each other. Terrance made a remark in front of the crowd that embarrassed Dwight, and he left extremely angry. Within minutes, Dwight returned. He had a shotgun. Dwight put the barrel of the gun against Terrance's chest. Everyone went silent. Over and over, Terrance dared Dwight to pull the trigger. Nothing happened. So Terrance went to grab the barrel. The gun went off. Dwight had blasted a hole through Terrance's chest. It didn't take long for Terrance to die. I know because I was 13 years old and I was there.

"Terrance had a great opportunity to make it out, go on to college, and get a good job. Instead, like many other guys I knew from my community, he chose to get involved in drinking and drugs. And Terrance, like others I grew up with, ended up dying a violent death before his life really even started."

* * *

It amazes me – and it also makes me sad – to think that Terrance and I walked along similar paths growing up but that our destinations ended up so very different. Terrance's life ended way too soon and was filled with tragedy and violence. As of today, my journey has been a successful one. I won't kid you; there were some tough times grow-ing up. And I learned many lessons the hard way. But I persevered, and today my life is filled with peace, joy, and happiness.

I want you to know that you're not destined to have a life like Terrance's. Even though you might be in the thick of a mess right now, there's hope. You can make it out and build a wonderful life for yourself. Always keep in mind that you have choices. It may not seem like it now but trust me on this one. I know.

I had many of the same nasty things thrown at me that you might see every day. The difference was that I never lost hope. And, I made a choice. I made the choice to get out and succeed. I'll be straight: It wasn't easy. And it won't be easy for you. But if you want to realize your goals and dreams, you've got to want to change some things. And, you've got to want to change them very badly because there are temptations all around you that can steer you down the wrong path. They're in your community, your neighborhood, with your friends – even in your home.

Experience is one of life's best teachers. One great way to learn is to seek out and listen to those older and wiser than you who have succeeded. Please think of me as one of those people; one of the voices of experience. Guys, my only desire here is to pass on to you what I've learned on my journey so that your journey might be a little less bumpy than mine.

Everyday, you face difficult issues. Things like racism, poverty, pressures, loneliness, and others can weigh you down and create a burden so heavy that you simply give up and give in. Before you know it, you're living a life filled with fear and emptiness. But these things can be overcome! And I know you can overcome them! Why? Because I did.

One of the first steps in overcoming obstacles is getting the right information. This allows you to change the way you think about difficult issues in your life. I'm not telling you something new here, but there's a lot of bad information out there that guys get from friends and others in the community.

One of the keys to growth and success is knowledge. Knowledge can help you overcome just about any obstacle out there. Getting the right information and correcting or adjusting the way you think about and view an obstacle is crucial in helping you to reach your goals and dreams.

I want to set the record straight. I want you to be armed with the right information. So, I'm going to give you different, positive ways to think about things that usually get you down. Much of what I'm going to talk about was used by others who succeeded and they passed it on to me. Some things I learned along the way.

We're also going to talk about solutions. I'm going to introduce to you different things that you can do to overcome some of the negative influences that you face every day.

These solutions are all about taking action. Long ago, people older and wiser than me taught me that the only thing any of us can really control in life is how we behave and how we act. This is most important when we are faced with difficulties involving people, places, and situations. In these tough times, it's important that you learn to choose positive ways to act and react. And, how you act on and react to issues like poverty, racism, feelings of worthlessness, and others will have a huge effect on whether or not you succeed.

At the beginning of every chapter in this book is a quote from a famous African American man, and a little about his history, so that you can begin to learn more about how others like you, under extraordinarily difficult circumstances, succeeded. There also are some questions at the end of every chapter. These will allow you to reflect on how you can change your thinking and actions – and how you can begin to learn how to overcome obstacles.

You guys are important to me and many others. You are the future. And I want every one of you to have a fighting chance of realizing your goals and dreams like I had. So, let's go! Let's begin a new journey together – one that's filled with hope and solutions.

"If my mind can conceive it, and my heart can believe it, I know I can achieve it."

Jesse Jackson
Political Leader, Clergyman, and Civil Rights Activist
(Born 1941)

Born and raised in a poor family, Jackson worked hard in school and earned a scholarship to college. After graduation, Jackson pursued postgraduate work at the Chicago Theological Seminary and was ordained a Baptist minister in 1968. Jackson became active in the civil rights movement and was a close associate of Dr. Martin Luther King, Jr. Jackson founded Operation PUSH (People United to Save Humanity), an organization to combat racism. Since 1986 he has been president of the National Rainbow Coalition, an independent political organization aimed at uniting different groups like racial minorities, the poor, peace activists, and environmentalists. In 1984 and 1988, Jackson, an effective public speaker, campaigned for the Democratic nomination for president, becoming the first African American to contend seriously for that office.

Chapter 1

Love

Love is a word that's thrown around very loosely and carelessly by people in our society, especially by boys to girls. I believe it's because many don't know what love truly means. You have your own definition of love, one that has been taught and modeled to you by family, friends, others in your community, and society. What concerns me is that many of you have gotten bad information. So, let's set the record straight and get you good information about love. But before we do that, let's go over some of the faulty information that's out there about love and get an understanding about how it got there in the first place.

Today, most boys have two misconceptions about love. The first one is that love is mainly physical. What do I mean by physical? I mean sex and physical displays of affection (hugging, touching, kissing).

Let's go over how this misconception is formed.

Guys, you are bombarded daily by messages and images from music lyrics, music videos, movies, TV, and other media. These have a tremendous influence over how you develop and shape your perception and definition of love. Let's keep it real here: Most of the images and messages you see and hear are about sex. The message you are getting is that if you love a girl, then the way you express it is through sex or some other physical display of affection. And, you're told that you need to do this at a young age and early on in a relationship.

I'm here to tell you that this is not love. I know these messages and images come to you at a dizzying rate and that it may be hard to believe that what these people are saying is wrong. But trust me, they are way off base!

Musicians (rap, R&B, rock, and others) and movie makers are out for one thing and one thing only: to try and get you to spend your money on what they are selling. Simply put, they want you to buy something. And these artists spend a lot of time and effort trying to understand and figure out how to get you to do this.

One thing the media's learned is that sex sells to kids your age. These artists don't care about you and the negative influence their messages and images have over you. All they care about is their bottom line. They'll do whatever it takes to get as much of your money as they can.

On top of all this, many of you may be getting pressure from your friends and even adult males in your community to become a "player." If this is happening to you, the message you're getting is that it's cool to have sex. Other boys and adult males may give you respect when you're a "player." But listen to me carefully: Being a "player" has nothing to do with love.

Let's go over some of the negative things that are likely to happen when you have the "player" mentality, when you think love is mostly about sex. You run the risk of getting a sexually transmitted disease (or STD), HIV, and/or AIDS. You run the risk of getting a girl pregnant and feeling pressured to get married young. Also, you may end up having to pay child support, which can dramatically affect your financial future.

So let's play the tape all the way forward. These are all very real consequences that result from faulty perceptions of love, and these faulty perceptions can spell disaster for you. Any one of these negative consequences puts you further away from your goals and dreams.

The second misconception that many of you might have about love is that it's "material." Let me paint a picture for you. Here's what many of you may end up thinking you must do to show or receive love: accumulate a lot of material things, make yourself fit a certain physical image, and most of all keep a bunch of money in your pocket. You may be led to believe that this is what it takes for others to want to love you, and that lavishing material things on someone is how you show love to others.

Guys, having clothes, a nice car, money in your pocket, and giving gifts to others are not wrong or bad in and of themselves. It becomes wrong when your motivation behind accumulating these things is to seduce someone into sleeping with you or having sex with you. For many boys, the message society is sending is that if you have all these things, you'll get the girl.

This kind of thinking just isn't true. I know. I've seen many guys choose this way of life, and I've even tried it myself. It's a life filled with deception and unhappiness. When you try to have a relationship with a girl and lead her to think that all she has to do to get her hopes and dreams to come true is to be with you – and sex becomes part of that too – it only hurts both of you in many different ways. This kind of thinking is wrong for many reasons.

Here are two that I want to share with you:

1. Trying to portray a "player" image over a long period of time puts some serious pressure on boys to make and keep money so they can carry on this image. Competition to be number one is fierce. This is likely to lead to shortcuts. And you know what I'm talking about here: selling drugs, stealing, or joining gangs to make fast cash. Involvement in any one of these things takes you further away from true success and puts you closer to trouble, jail, and even death. Or, sometimes boys will overwork themselves at a young age to make money instead of enjoying all that comes with being a kid or teenager.

2. When a girl is led to believe that love is all about a person giving her things, then she is going to expect more and more. And, if you want to keep her, you've got to keep it coming – and that can be extremely difficult. There may be someone who comes along who has more things to offer. And, when the girl thinks love is "what can you give me," then she may leave you for someone else who "has it going on." And trust me, the word will get out that you fell short. This can lead to hurt, pain, and anger for you. Does any of that sound like love to you? Me neither!

Let me give all this to you straight: Love is not physical only and love is not just about giving material things either. Most importantly, sex as a way of showing love is one of the last things that should happen in a relationship – and I'm talking about two well-prepared, married adults. Love also is not about trying to use and manipulate another person in order to satisfy your desire or wants. Why? Because when one person loves another, he or she should not lead the other person into doing something wrong or hurtful.

So, what is love? I believe it's a healthy person-to-person relationship where there is respect for each other and knowledge that the other person is someone you can trust; someone who will help keep you safe and on the right track to becoming a better person.

In order to love someone in this way, you first have to learn to love yourself. Face it fellas, you can't give away something you haven't got. And if you haven't developed a healthy sense of who you are and come to love and respect yourself, then it's impossible to experience real love with someone else. It's like this: if you love a girl, you won't do things to harm her. And if she loves you, she won't don't things to harm you either.

Now, let's talk about some solutions. Let's dis-

cuss some ways you can learn to love and respect
yourself at all levels – physically, emotionally, intel-
lectually, spiritually. Spending time learning how to
love and respect yourself takes your focus off of the
physical and material misconceptions of love. Also,
it allows you to prepare yourself for understanding
how to pass on real love to another person when
the time is right.

The following tips will help you learn how to
focus on ways to make yourself a better person, one
who is capable of giving and receiving love.

- Get involved in different activities that interest
  you at school, at church, and in your community. Get your mind and body away from the traps
  and dangers of sex.

- Get involved in sports.

- Spend time being social and building healthy
  relationships with other positive young people.

- Don't let your environment and society define
  who you are. Discover this for yourself with the
  help of trusted, caring adults (parents, relatives,
  teachers, coaches, and others).

- Create a healthy lifestyle by cultivating your
  mind. Read, take care of your schoolwork, diver-
  sify yourself by getting involved in activities that

are new and challenge you (clubs at school, a church-sponsored youth program, etc.).

- Seek out others to help you develop a love for the intellectual part of you. A teacher, parent, relative, or coach can introduce you to a world filled with subjects and ideas that you might have never known existed.

- Be courageous and don't allow yourself to be pigeon-holed as an athlete or a player. You can be so much more than that!

- Take time to learn about and experience different people, cultures, and places. This can happen through involvement in school, church, and community groups.

- Take care of yourself physically by staying away from alcohol, drugs, gangs, and sex.

- Seek out people – both adults and other kids – who are positive, caring, and want to help you.

- Go to church. And get involved when you go! Most of all, pray. Pray for yourself and others. Trust me, prayer works.

I think you get the idea here. There are many other things you can do to focus on bettering yourself and learning to love and respect you. It's not an easy road to choose. There will be temptations and pressures all around that you'll have to fight off. I know that because my journey was filled with these same challenges.

Guys, it's easy to follow the crowd. But a crowd filled with negativity and danger has no room for love – just self-centeredness and harm.

As you learn to love and respect yourself, you will become a happy, well-rounded, and balanced person. And when the time comes to love someone, you will be ready and capable of giving and receiving real love – a true love of the spirit, where you respect others enough to do them no harm.

What Do You Think?

1. Name and describe the two common misconceptions about love.

_____

_____

_____

_____

_____

_____

_____

_____

_____

_____

_____

_____

2. What is your definition of "real" love?

3. Did your definition of love change after reading this chapter? How?

4. What are some ways that were discussed in the chapter that can help you become a better person, one who's more capable of giving and receiving real love?

"People might not get all they work for in this world, but they must certainly work for all they get."

Frederick Douglass
American Abolitionist
(1817 - 1895)

The son of a black slave, Douglass escaped from slavery on his second attempt. During the time he was a slave, Douglass learned to read and write. In 1845, he published a book, *Narrative of the Life of Frederick Douglass*, that went on to become a classic in American literature as well as a primary resource about slavery. Fearing capture from his old slave master, Douglass spent several years in England and Ireland, returning to the United States in 1847 after English friends purchased his freedom. Douglass established the *North Star*, an anti-slavery newspaper, and edited it for 17 years in the cause to end slavery. He favored using political methods over violence to bring about change. Douglass was one of the most important human rights leaders of the 19th century. His speaking and writing abilities helped move him into a leadership role in the anti-slavery movement, and he became the first African American citizen to hold high rank in the U.S. government.

Chapter 2

Poverty

When I work with and teach kids, especially African American kids, the issue of poverty comes up often. During our discussions, kids talk about poverty mainly in terms of the material things they don't have. Simply put, they think poverty means a lack of money or not having enough material things.

Now don't get me wrong here. I don't want to diminish the fact that many of these kids do come from some very tough, poor backgrounds. They might come from impoverished communities and neighborhoods or from families on welfare – and they don't have a lot. My point here is that kids today relate the issue of poverty directly with money – or lack of money. They focus on the things their community or family does not have.

This kind of thinking can have a dramatic effect on you and your chance of realizing your goals and dreams. When your main focus is on run-down homes or buildings, parks and playgrounds that need to be tended to and fixed up, or schools in need of repair, it starts to weigh on your mind and how you think about your situation. Over time, it can lead to an "I can't" way of thinking. What this means is that all these things become mental roadblocks or reasons why you think you can't succeed.

Sure, money and poverty are linked together. I grew up in a poor community that was run down in many areas, and I lived in a home where we struggled to have enough money to live on. But I never thought I lived in poverty. And I certainly never thought that a lack of money could keep me from realizing my goals. Why? Because I thought about poverty in a different way, one that I'd like to share with you.

I believe that a "poverty of hope and faith" is real poverty. It's the worst kind of poverty, much worse than not having money or enough material things in your life.

Now, what do I mean by a "poverty of hope and faith"? Before we get into that, let's first talk about what I mean by hope and faith. Hope is the vision you have in your heart and mind about how you can contribute to those around you in positive ways – whether it's as a doctor, teacher, nurse, businessman, parent, or whatever your goal in life is.

Faith is a belief that your hopes (or goals) can come to be and that you can take the necessary steps to make them come true. Now, the action part of faith is real important here. Why? Simply put, faith without action is nothing. Let me explain: You can have great hope and a strong belief in yourself and your ability to succeed, but if you don't take the steps needed to make your goals reality, then faith is irrelevant. And, you certainly won't achieve your hopes and goals.

So let's talk about how all this relates to how you think about poverty. When you have a "poverty of hope and faith," it means you've given up. You've allowed issues on the outside (lack of money and material stuff) to influence the spirit inside of you in a dramatically negative way. When this happens, kids throw in the towel and give in to the destructive things around them.

But it doesn't have to be this way for you! You can learn to build an abundance of hope and faith in yourself. Let me share with you some things I learned along the way, things that will help you strengthen and keep alive the hope and faith you have in yourself and your ability to succeed despite what's around you.

- Don't just focus on problems; think about and focus on solutions. Whenever you encounter a problem, ask yourself, "What's the solution here and how can I be part of it?" Focus your thoughts on how you can get involved in the solution. What actions can you take to make things right? If all this isn't clear to you, ask for help from those trusted, positive adults around you – parents, family members, teachers, coaches, pastors, and others.

- **Persevere as you encounter life's obstacles.** Ignore and get away from those people who hate, criticize, and complain. Don't allow those around you who believe that poverty can't be overcome to pull you back. Instead, keep walking forward; keep taking the right steps that lead straight toward your goals.

- **Inventory and use the resources around you.** There are many people (parents, family members, teachers, coaches, pastors, mentors) and organizations (schools, churches, community centers, YMCAs, Boys and Girls Clubs) out there that are ready, willing, and able to help you succeed – and most don't cost a penny. Seek these people and organizations out. Let them know that you want to be involved, ask for help, and be willing to do whatever it takes to reach your goals.

- **Be honest, vocal, and upfront with people about what you want to do.** But, make sure they are the right people. Make sure they are people who care and support you, and that they are in a position to be able to provide help. Share with them your goals, hopes, and dreams. Try it! You'll be surprised at how many people will be willing to help you achieve. I know I was!

- **Make connections outside your immediate surroundings.** This means getting involved in things like school-sponsored activities, church youth groups, and community-based projects and programs. This allows you to meet and get to know others who might be able to help you. Or, they might be able to introduce you to someone who can have a huge impact on helping you reach your goals. This is called "networking," and it happens all the time. But you have to make it happen! These people won't come looking for you; you have to find them.

- **Read about, explore, and honor your heritage.** Go to the library and read about those in the African American culture who've succeeded. Our culture is filled with people who fought through incredible poverty and reached their goals and dreams. These people can inspire you to do the same. If you don't know where to start, ask a family member, teacher, or librarian. They would love to help you learn more about our culture.

- **Go to church and pray daily.** Take the time to talk to God and thank him for the wonderful people, places, and things that you do have. This kind of positive action helps you focus on all the good that you have in your life. And talk to Him about your troubles. Ask Him for help. He'll come through for you if you believe and live your life the right way. I know because He's been there for me!

Guys, let's keep it real: When your focus is on things you don't have (money or material things), you blind yourself to all the positive people, places, and things in your life that can help you succeed. So, shift your focus! Look at and be grateful for all the gifts you do have. When you do this, you'll find that your eyes are now open and you're able to see that no matter what your situation is, hope, faith, and positive actions on your part will take you where you dream to go.

What Do You Think?

1. What does it mean to have a "poverty of hope and faith"? How is this different from the way most people define poverty?

2. Describe all the ways that you are "rich" in your life today.

_____

_____

_____

_____

_____

_____

_____

_____

_____

_____

_____

_____

_____

3. What are some ways you can strengthen your
   hope and faith in yourself and your ability to
   succeed?

4. What does Frederick Douglass's quote at the beginning of the chapter tell you about how to look at and handle poverty?

_____

_____

_____

_____

_____

_____

_____

_____

_____

_____

_____

_____

_____

_____

"Racism is not an excuse to not do the best you can."

Arthur Ashe
Professional Tennis Player
(1943 - 1993)

Arthur Ashe began playing tennis at the age
of 7 in a neighborhood park. With hard work
and dedication, he became a gifted tennis player.
Ashe had tremendous success in national junior
tournaments, and the University of California at Los
Angeles (UCLA) offered him a tennis scholarship.
He graduated from college and then played
professional tennis. During his career, Ashe won
many tournaments at all levels, including many major
championships. He was often the first African
American to win these events. After retiring from
tennis, Ashe remained an active spokesman on
social issues, including race relations and AIDS,
until his death.

Chapter 3

Racism

When you're young, the people and environment around you have a tremendous influence on your beliefs and attitudes toward many issues, including race and how you perceive other cultures. This is no different for you today than it was for me when I was your age.

Kids learn how trusted and respected adults think and feel about various issues by listening to and watching them. Their words and actions provide you with information that helps you form beliefs and attitudes on many different topics. Most times, kids take on the very same beliefs and attitudes as those providing them with the information.

The concern I have is that when the information is faulty it usually leads to some pretty messed up thinking and actions. I've found that this is the case when it comes to the way many young African

American boys view race and people from different cultures, especially the white culture.

When I was your age, the information I got about other cultures, specifically the white culture, was very negative. The message I got and the message that many of you are getting today is the same: That the white culture controls money and jobs. And, because they control these two things, they control everything – including you. This kind of thinking has been around our culture for a long, long time – and it's just plain wrong. If you want to succeed, it's time for you to change the way you think about this.

Guys, let's keep it real. More people in the white culture may be in better positions regarding hiring people for jobs or better off financially than African Americans. Whether or not this is true is really unimportant. What is important for you to realize is this: Other people and other cultures do *not* control you or your destiny. That control belongs to you and to you only!

We are all human beings created by God. All of us, no matter the color of our skin, are capable of choosing to do good or evil. So, the thinking that people from another culture control you and your opportunities to succeed just doesn't fly. There are far too many success stories of African Americans achieving and doing great things in local communities, in our nation, and around the world for this kind of thinking to be true.

Fellas, it all comes down to each and every person within cultures. Some people choose to do good things in this world and some choose to be involved in bad things that hurt other people. This is true in any culture; it's not something unique to one culture only. As a matter of fact, I've seen people within the African American culture choose to do much more harm to fellow African Americans than a person from any other culture would do.

I'm not saying that racism doesn't exist in the world. Many of us have seen, read, and experienced it in our own lives. But, I've come to learn that most racial discrimination today is isolated. It's more the exception than the rule. Racism happens because of the way an individual may think and act. It's not because society as a whole is racist. Today, there are many, many more people who are accepting of and supportive of other cultures than are not.

So, it's time to get beyond this way of thinking. It's just a mental roadblock to reaching your goals and dreams.

How can you change the way you think and act about racism? The following are some ways that I believe can help you overcome the obstacle that racism can be to your success.

- **If you come across racism – the kind that's real and "in your face" – don't let it deter you from your goals.** Continue to persevere! Keep on stepping toward success! This is what successful African Americans have done throughout our history when faced with real racism.

- **Sometimes the best way to deal with real racism is to go around it, not through it.** You have to decide whether or not it's a fight worth fighting. Many times, it's best to just keep on marching around a roadblock instead of spending lots of time and energy fighting through it. Don't delay your journey to success any longer than you have to! If you need help deciding what to do, go ask an adult that you trust and respect. Seek out advice from others who have succeeded. They'll be happy to help.

- **Don't worry or obsess about racism when it isn't there.** I've seen way too many kids sit around talking and complaining about racial discrimination, even when it's not part of their lives. This is a complete waste of time. If racism isn't there right in front of you blocking your path, then leave it alone! Don't allow yourself to get caught up with negative people who simply want to moan about something that's not even affecting them. Time is precious, so don't waste it on ghosts. Instead, spend your time doing the things needed to reach your goals and dreams.

- **When you do come across real racism, handle it in a "professional" manner.** By this I mean stay calm and deal with it in a peaceful way. For example, if racism happens to you in a restaurant, calmly ask to speak to the manager, tell him or her what happened, and don't go there anymore. Most often, that's the best you can do. Getting upset and yelling or arguing will get you nowhere. Be a person who handles difficult situations like racism in a sensible and professional way.

- **Focus on what you can control.** That means you and your actions. Ask yourself every day, "What have I done to move toward my goals?" Focus your mind on positive daily actions that will lead you to success. When you're busy taking positive steps each day, you won't have time to think about possible obstacles like racism.

- **Reach out to positive kids in your school, church, or neighborhood that are from other cultures.** Get to know them as individuals first. Many times, you'll find that friendships will develop. When this happens, you begin to learn for yourself what people from other cultures are all about. You'll get to gather your own information, form your own opinions, and draw your own conclusions about others who are different from you. This allows you to overcome the negative power of racism because you are connecting and networking with positive people from different cultures. Also, this is a time when you can inform and teach others about the African American culture. Interacting positively with others from different cultures is one of the best ways to get good information.

- **Learn to take "No" for an answer, but don't always take "No" for an answer.** When striving to reach goals, you're going to need the help of others. So first off, don't be afraid to ask for help. Most times, you'll find people of all cultures who are more than willing to help you if you just reach out and ask. But there will be times when people tell you "No"; that they can't help you, for whatever reason. When this happens, politely say "thanks" and move on to the next person. Be persistent! It's the only way any person of any race succeeds.

- **Read about and study how others dealt with and overcame racism.** Our culture is overflowing with men and women who persevered and succeeded despite tremendous racial discrimination. The first thing that you'll find is that your path to success is much easier today than it was for others in the past. Second, these success stories inspire you to persevere. Finally, you'll learn that those who overcame racial discrimination and succeeded did so in a peaceful, professional way. In the long run, dealing with racism with hate and violence only leads to disastrous outcomes.

- **Opportunity comes to those who are prepared.** This means that you need to take positive actions each day to prepare yourself. By doing this, you're better able to recognize and grasp opportunity when it comes your way. So, spend time each day doing positive things that move you toward your goals. Stay away from negative influences that move you away from success.

- **Remember that God loves *all* people.** He made all of us equal. And, He wants us to love and help each other. So pray to Him. Ask God to help the person who suffers from racism and pray for those individuals who are part of the problem. Also, always remember the Golden Rule: Treat others as you would want to be treated. This means all people in all cultures. When you apply this rule to your own life, you'll find that things almost always turn out for the best.

Guys, let's keep it real. Today, racism is not as much of a major roadblock in your journey to success as it was for African Americans in the past. Sure, it can get better and there are still some things to work out. But remember those who came before you, like Malcolm X. He grew up believing that the best way to deal with racism was through hate and violence. But, through many different experiences as an adult, Malcolm X came full circle and his philosophy on dealing with racism was completely transformed. He came to believe that racial discrimination was best handled peacefully and professionally.

People like Malcolm X and Dr. Martin Luther King Jr. died defending their beliefs and ensuring a better future for you. Now, your responsibility is to keep their hope, message, and memories alive. Take actions that your forefathers would be proud and approve of. Be a leader and show others how it's done!

What Do You Think?

1. How do many people develop racist thoughts, attitudes, and actions?

2. In what ways are you in control of your life and your ability to succeed?

3. What are some new ways you can think about
   and act on racism that will help you succeed?

4. In Arthur Ashe's quote at the beginning of the chapter, he talks about not using racism as an excuse. What does this mean to you?

_____

_____

_____

_____

_____

_____

_____

_____

_____

_____

_____

_____

"The future belongs to
those who prepare for
it today."

Malcolm X
African American Leader
and Muslim Minister
(1925 - 1965)

Growing up, Malcolm saw his home burned to the
ground by the Ku Klux Klan, a white supremacist
group. Two years later, his father was murdered,
and Malcolm's mother was subsequently placed
in a mental institution. Malcolm spent many of
his childhood years in detention homes. Later, he
spent time in prison for burglary. While there,
Malcolm converted to the Black Muslim faith
(Nation of Islam), which professed that blacks were
superior to whites and that white people were evil.
Following his release from prison, Malcolm became
involved in the civil rights movement. At that time,
he believed in black separatism, black pride, and
black self-dependence. He also supported the use

of violence, especially when it came to protecting oneself. Because of these beliefs, Malcolm's leadership was rejected by most civil rights leaders who believed in nonviolence as the way to deal with racial injustice. In 1964, after a pilgrimage to Mecca, Malcolm changed his views, declaring that he no longer believed whites to be innately evil and acknowledging that blacks and whites could live together in brotherhood. As a result of these changed beliefs, he was assassinated. Malcolm's transformation, however, continues to inspire many African Americans today.

Chapter 4

Worthlessness

A feeling of worthlessness means that a person thinks and feels that he's not a valuable human being or member of society. When someone, especially a kid, develops this kind of thinking and feels this way, it's devastating to his chances for success in life. That's why I want to talk to you about this important topic.

Kids develop feelings of worthlessness in different ways. It can happen inside or outside your home. But, it's most damaging when it comes from inside your home. Unfortunately, home is where most kids begin to develop their feelings of worthlessness. Many times, it's planted in their minds at a very young age by parents and other important family members who don't provide support in words or actions.

Kids may be told that they are "lazy," "no good," "won't amount to anything," and are bombarded with other negative messages and labels. These are verbal assaults coming from "trusted" adults that kids don't know how to handle. As these harmful messages and labels are repeated over time, kids end up believing what these people are saying about them and they allow these negative messages and labels to define who they are as a person.

Once feelings of worthlessness are pounded into your mind, it affects how you see yourself and, ultimately, how you think and act. You might start figuring that since you're destined for no good, why even try. Or, you may believe that since you're never going to be successful, why not give in to the many temptations around you – alcohol, drugs, sex, etc.

Another danger with this kind of thinking is that many kids start looking for love, affection, and feelings of worth and belonging in the wrong places, like in gangs and with drug dealers. Fellas, let's keep it real: Being part of a gang or getting involved with a drug dealer isn't the answer. These negative activities only give you false feelings of value and purpose and, ultimately, lead you in the opposite direction of your goals.

Okay, we've discussed what the problem is and some of the dangers that can come from letting feelings of worthlessness take over your mind and actions. Knowing all of this is important in helping you overcome this obstacle. Now, let's start talking about solutions! The following are some practical and useful things you can do to successfully deal with feelings of worthlessness.

- **Don't allow others to define who and what you are.** Always stay steady and confident in your abilities to succeed and to define who you are and what you want to be. Remember: Don't let what anyone has to say get in the way of you being successful!

- **Assess your strengths and weaknesses.** Write down the things you do well, along with the things you need to improve on. Be fair and honest when you do this. Also, it's a good idea to go to positive and trusted adults to get their feedback on the list you developed. Listen to what they have to say; it's always good to bounce things off others as a reality check. Once you've discovered what it is you do well, go for it! Make sure that it's something you're good at, enjoy doing, and benefits others. When these three things are in place, you can be sure you're headed down the right path.

- **Work on your weaknesses.** All of us have areas in our lives where we can improve. Getting better in these areas gives us a much better chance at reaching our goals. Positive personal growth and feeling good about yourself involve knowing your talents – that's a given. However, it also means that you come to understand, accept, and improve on areas where you're not so good. Many times, you'll find that your greatest sense of accomplishment and feelings of satisfaction come from the positive strides you make in overcoming your weaknesses. Trying to do things better is a lifelong endeavor that allows you to become a better person.

- **Put your strengths to positive use.** When you do this, you'll find that you have the ability to be a positive influence on others and the world around you. For example, if you are good at and like to draw, don't waste it in a negative way like painting graffiti on buildings. Instead, ask what you can do at school, in the community, and at your church to put your time and artistic talent to use in a constructive manner. Helping others is one of the surest and quickest ways for you to create positive thoughts and feelings about who you are.

- **Use positive self-talk.** This means that you tell yourself over and over that you're a good person who is capable of doing great things for yourself and others. Do this every day! You might find it helpful to write down positive things to tell yourself, especially for those times when life's not going so well. It's only through practice like this that you can get rid of the negative thoughts and feelings that you might have about yourself. Let's face it guys, sometimes we have to be our own cheerleaders. Positive self-talk is a great way to keep yourself motivated and on the march toward your goals.

- **Choose to hang around positive people.** People who are negative and don't support you can drag you down. That's why it's very important to steer clear of these kinds of kids and adults. Instead, spend your time with people who are upbeat, optimistic, supportive, and doing worthwhile things. Seek them out! You need to be with people who tell and show you that you are worthy and valuable. If these negative people are at home, the situation is a bit more difficult. My suggestion is to just let their negative messages and comments go in one ear and out the other. I know this can be tough to do, but many times ignoring and walking away is a better option than confrontation. Always remember that the only person you can control and change is you. If you do feel the need to say something to the person, wait for a neutral time and let the person know in a calm way that his or her negative messages and comments are hurtful to you. It may help the situation or it may not, but at least you'll feel better by taking some action and making your feelings known.

- **Ask for help.** Be strong and let those positive people in your life know what it is that you want to do. Ask them for help and guidance. We all need the assistance of others to succeed. Just do it! You'll be pleasantly surprised at their willingness to reach out and help you achieve.

- **Choose to hang out in places where positive things are going on.** Look to your school and church, the Boys Club and YMCA, and other community-based support organizations. These are all safe and supportive places where you can find tons of positive activities that will help prepare you for success. Stay away from hanging out on the street corner. There is nothing positive going on there that will help you realize your goals.

- **Talk to a trusted and caring person about your feelings.** It's very easy to get frustrated and angry when people close to you are unsupportive and negative. Many kids choose to bottle up these hurtful feelings. But, over time, they are bound to come out. And many times, this pent-up anger and frustration is taken out on innocent people like teachers, mentors, coaches, friends, and others. The best thing to do when you feel angry and frustrated is to talk to trusted and caring adults. Seek them out as soon as possible and tell them how you're feeling. Don't let these negative feelings build up inside you. Many times, just getting it off your chest is all you need to do to leave it behind and continue moving forward.

- **Read and learn about successful African Americans.** Many people in our culture have succeeded despite experiencing words and actions that created obstacles that seemed insurmountable. But time and time again, these people kept moving forward because they believed in themselves. And, they knew that what they were attempting to accomplish was of value. They refused to let the negative words and actions of others get them down and deter them from their path to success. There are many books and websites where you can read about these people. (If you need help finding them, ask a librarian or an adult who is knowledgeable about our culture's history.) Not only is it inspirational to read about these people but it also can teach you new and better ways to go about achieving your goals and dreams.

- **Don't give people an opportunity to label you.** I'm going to say this very simply: Don't do or say negative things that give people reasons to label you as a certain kind of person. For example, if you hang out with people in gangs or with kids who do drugs, you'll be guilty by association and get labeled as a "gangbanger" or "druggie." Once you get a label, it's difficult to get rid of it – and you may end up believing that it's true. The solution to all this is pretty simple: Make good choices, take the right actions, say nice things to others, and treat people well. They in turn are more likely to treat you in the same way.

- **Don't compare yourself to others.** Always remember that you do things well and that others also do things well. Sometimes others might even do things better than you. But that's okay. Don't get caught up in comparisons and wanting to be something you're not, or being jealous or envious of others. That will surely lead to feelings of worthlessness. Instead, be comfortable with your abilities, interests, and who you are.

- **Look to prayer and your faith for strength.** God doesn't make trash. He values, loves, respects, and accepts you for exactly who you are. He put the "seal of approval" on you as a human being from the very start. That's why it's important for you to build a relationship with God through prayer and going to church. When you go to church and pray, you hear about and experience God's love for you. Church is a positive place where you can find comfort and strength, especially when times are tough.

Guys, let's keep it real: Don't let other people's words or actions determine who you are and what you want to become. These things are up to you – and to you only. Once you've determined the best path to success, never let the negative words, messages, and actions of others steer you from your path. Be strong and always persevere!

What Do You Think?

1. Have you ever had bad feelings about yourself? What do you think caused those feelings?

2. Explain how feelings of worthlessness can be dangerous to your life and success.

_____

_____

_____

_____

_____

_____

_____

_____

_____

_____

_____

_____

_____

_____

3. What are some ways to overcome feelings of worthlessness? In what ways can you apply these to your life?

4. Ask an older relative (parent, grandparent, aunt, uncle, etc.) about what he or she thinks Malcolm X would have said about how to overcome obstacles in your life. Write the response here.

_____

_____

_____

_____

_____

_____

_____

_____

_____

_____

_____

_____

_____

"There are no secrets to success. Don't waste your time looking for them. Success is the result of perfection, hard work, learning from failure, loyalty to those for whom you work, and persistence."

Colin Powell
U.S. Army General
and Government Official
(Born 1937)

The son of Jamaican immigrants, Powell grew up in the Harlem and South Bronx sections of New York City. In college, he served in the Reserve Officers' Training Corps (ROTC). After joining the army, Powell served in the Vietnam War and later rose to the rank of four-star general. Powell was appointed to many top government positions, including Chairman of the U.S. Joint Chiefs of Staff (1989–93) and Secretary of State (2000-04). He was the first African American to hold either position.

Chapter 5

The American Dream

One of the greatest things about living in the United States is the freedom we all have to follow our dreams. If you can dream it, you have the opportunity in America to make it happen. But, it's got to be your dream.

The problem I see for many African American boys is that other people are defining the "American Dream" for them. It gets risky for you when this happens. Why? Because it's hard to be successful trying to live up to someone else's expectations and standards. Those of you who are in this kind of situation are likely to think and feel that the dreams and goals others set for you are unattainable, either because they are unrealistic or are not something you want to do. This is why you, and not someone else, should ultimately decide what your dreams and goals are.

Another problem I see in today's world is that the American Dream is greatly influenced by the media. MTV, BET, ESPN, and other media glamorize the lives of musicians, entertainers, athletes, and others who are enormously rich and famous. The message that's being sent to you and many others is that the American Dream is all about money (and lots of it!), fancy cars, huge mansions, expensive jewelry, beautiful women, and sex. And that anything short of having all these things is not living the America Dream.

Guys, this kind of thinking is wrong. The American Dream is not about the fame and fortune that might come from being a professional athlete, entertainer, or celebrity. For most of us, these goals are simply unrealistic. I was a very good basketball player growing up, good enough to play in college. But I was still way short of having the physical gifts needed to play professionally. Only a handful of people have these kinds of natural gifts.

Okay, now that I've explained what the American Dream is not, let's talk about what it is. I believe that the American Dream is your own personal vision and hope for your future, and your ability to be able to pursue it. Also, I believe it's very important that whatever it is you dream and pursue contributes positively to others and the world around you. Simply put, it's all about you coming to a realistic decision about what you want to do with your life, the kind of person you want to be, and having the freedom to make it happen.

The beauty of the American Dream is that it can be anything. It can be big or small. And it can come in all shapes and sizes. Your American Dream may have a big house, fancy cars, and lots of money in it, and it may not. It may include lots of higher education, and it may not. You may want to own a small business (a barbershop or auto shop) or you may not. I do believe, however, that in every American Dream, there should be the freedom to think it and pursue it, and it should benefit others and society.

The American Dream is unique to each person. This means that it won't be the same for everyone. Some of you may want to be doctors or lawyers. Others might want to be teachers or social workers. Still others may want to be storeowners or carpenters. The options are limitless! The important point here is that as long as your American Dream is something you're good at, something you like and want to do, and it contributes positively to others, then it's worth pursuing.

Ultimately, it's up to you to decide what your dreams and goals are. Don't get caught up in what others think you should do or be. Guys, you are driving the bus; you ultimately decide what your American Dream is.

Let's talk about some important things to consider as you go about discovering your personal American Dream.

- **Stay strong.** Be what *you* want to be. Follow the dreams you want to follow and don't let others or life's circumstances get in the way of your dreams. Stand tall and don't give in to the pressures of others who want you to be something you don't want to be.

- **Assess your strengths.** Honestly and thoroughly evaluate the things you're good at, enjoy doing, and that have a positive effect on others and the world around you. Sit down and write these things out. Determine what direction you want to take and then go for it! Just be sure that whatever you choose to do is something that's realistic as far as your ability and desire to make it happen – and that it's a positive contribution. If you need help with all of this (and many of you will; I know I did!), go to a trusted and caring adult whose motivation is to help you succeed.

- **Allow others to help guide you.** Always be teachable. At your age, choices and decisions

about what you want to do in life aren't easy
to make, and they usually aren't very clear.
Many times, we need the advice and strength
of others (parents, relatives, teachers, coaches,
mentors, and other wise, caring adults) to
help us wade through all the possibilities and
options. When you're with the right guide, the
whole decision-making process can be much
easier, and you're much more likely to arrive at
a better answer.

- **Remember guys: The American Dream isn't
  about who accumulates the most "stuff."** That
  way of thinking is selfish and greedy, and a sure
  way to end up lonely and unhappy. Be careful.
  Don't believe what marketers tell you about the
  American Dream. They're just trying to make a
  buck off you by getting you to buy something.

- **The world around you can be pretty tough and
  gloomy sometimes.** It needs more positive contri-
  butions from people like you. When you do this,
  you are helping others and you'll find that you feel
  great about yourself and what you're doing.

- **Take action.** You can dream all you want. But
  in order to achieve your dreams, you must
  take actions every day that move you forward.
  Create a plan of daily actions and follow it!
  This is called a "blueprint to success." Realizing

dreams takes hard work and perseverance. But it's all worth it in the end!

- **Make connections with people who can help you take steps toward your dreams and goals.** Identify people in your community or school who are successful and have the knowledge to help you on your way. Seek them out and ask for their help. If you're sincere and willing to do what it takes, you'll find that most of these people will be happy to help you.

- **Develop a strong spiritual foundation.** You can do this through daily prayer and going to church. A strong foundation in faith is essential to achieving positive outcomes in life. It gives us the power and strength to dream and to pursue those dreams. Faith can give you a vision of what is possible. Equally important, a strong faith gives you a safety net and support system for when times get tough. And they will. Dream chasing is tough work and there'll be setbacks. But God and those around you with a strong faith can give you the strength and courage to keep on moving forward.

- **Keep your focus squarely on your dreams and goals.** There is always something "fun" going on around you, especially with your friends. It's tempting to stop working and to just go have fun. You have to find a balance. Realizing your dreams and goals requires sacrifice. That means there will be times when have to tell your friends "No," that you can't go out and do something. This isn't easy to do at your age, but it's necessary if you want to succeed. One way to handle this is to make sure that you get all your work done before you go out and have fun with your friends. It really works! Try it.

- **Beware of dream killers.** What are dream killers? Negative people, jealous friends, drug dealers with the lure of fast cash, gangs, alcohol, drugs, and sex. All of these are supposed shortcuts or escapes. They are the quickest way to kill your dreams and goals. Avoid them at all costs! Instead, stay in the company of positive people who are doing positive things. You can find these people in your school, community, and church. When you get in with the right group, you get encouragement, support, and guidance.

- **Read and learn about successful people, those who've attained their American Dream.** Honor your won heritage and culture, but don't limit your reading and learning to just African Americans. American history is filled with people of all colors who have reached their dreams despite the odds. By doing this, you'll learn more about how to succeed and find inspiration for your own journey. Many people just like you have achieved their American Dream. Go find out exactly how they did it!

- **Be creative.** Most times, you have to work with what's right in front of you. Find new and creative ways to get the job done. Don't spend any time making up reasons why it can't be done. Instead, talk to others about how you can use the resources and people around you to your advantage.

- **Ask those around you who have succeeded how they did it.** I'm serious; just go up and talk to them! Most people enjoy sharing with others how they attained their dreams and goals. And, don't be too proud to say, "I need some help." Instead, allow others to show you ways to be successful.

Guys, let's keep it real: Make your dreams and goals your own. Don't let others determine these things for you. Rather, seek out positive and caring people and allow them to guide you on your journey to success. Whatever your American Dream is, it can be accomplished. It will require hard work and sacrifice. But, once you reach your dream, there's no better feeling in the world!

What Do You Think?

1. After reading this chapter, what does the "American Dream" mean to you?

2. What is your American Dream?

_____

_____

_____

_____

_____

_____

_____

_____

_____

_____

_____

_____

_____

3. How are you going to achieve your goals
   and dreams?

4. Read Colin Powell's quote again from the beginning of this chapter. What qualities did he believe were needed to reach a goal? Which qualities do you have and which do you need to work on?

_____

_____

_____

_____

_____

_____

_____

_____

_____

_____

_____

_____

"I don't know the key
to success, but the key
to failure is trying to
please everybody."

--------------------- **Bill Cosby**
Comedian, Actor, and Producer
(Born 1937)

Bill Cosby rose to fame as a comedian and then
became the first African American actor to star
in a dramatic series on television. He has since
starred in several television series, most notably
the situation comedy "The Cosby Show," the most
popular program on American television during
the late 1980s. Cosby has won numerous Emmy
awards and written several best-selling books. He
is a member of the Television Hall of Fame, and has
received a presidential medal. Cosby has played a
major role in the development of a more positive
portrayal of African Americans on television.

Chapter 6

Pressure

I've had the opportunity to work with kids who are in recovery from drug and alcohol abuse, kids in prison who committed crimes because of gang involvement, and young kids who are already parents. They've all got extremely tough roads ahead of them, and they know it. They wish they could go back in time and change what happened. But they can't.

When these kids and I look back at how they got to where they are now, they all talk about the pressure they felt to use, join a gang, or have sex. When we discuss "why" they felt the pressure to get involved in these negative things, it always goes back to relationships with others. These kids eventually gave into the pressures because they wanted to be involved in a relationship or be part of a group. They wanted to feel like they were part of something – to just belong. Many of you face these same pressures. I know I did when I was your age.

What I'm going to talk about is what I learned from these kids, and from my own experiences growing up. So, listen to the voices of experience. It'll help you make better choices and decisions when the pressure is on to belong or fit in.

In order to succeed, it's very important for you to build positive, healthy relationships and to leave behind the negative ones that can lead to destructive behaviors and activities. I know getting out of some relationships is a hard thing to do. It was tough for me. But when a relationship with a person or group of people involves pressure to use drugs or alcohol, join a gang, commit crimes, be violent, or have sex, it's not a relationship worth keeping.

Guys, let's keep it real: Trying to fit in by doing whatever it takes is foolish, and a sure path to heartache and failure. Don't let the desire to have a relationship with someone or to be involved with a group ruin your shot at success. You can still build and have positive relationships that don't involve negative pressures. This is an important part of anyone's success. Let's talk about how you can go about doing this.

- **Stay focused on your future.** Always look at what you do and who you hang with in terms of how it will affect what you want to do with your life. Don't allow yourself to get sucked into a negative relationship with a person or group just because you want to fit in. Giving into the pressures of a negative relationship will steer you away from success. So always keep your eyes on the prize!

- **Assess the health of your relationship with individuals and groups.** Look at these relationships with clear eyes. If there are negative or unhealthy pressures that come with a relationship, then it's time to cut that relationship loose – no matter how cool or fun it might seem to be. When assessing relationships, ask yourself this simple question: "Are the things going on in this relationship healthy for me or not?" If you are honest with yourself, the answer will be easy.

- **Trust yourself and your instincts.** Do you ever get a strange feeling in your gut – and in your heart and head – when you say, do, or are involved with something that's negative or wrong? Me too. Most all of us do. Be sensitive to your internal feelings about people. And when an internal sense tells you that a relationship is unhealthy, negative, or wrong, you must be willing to separate from that person or group of people. Simply put, if you sense or see negative pressures in a relationship, get out!

- **Be courageous.** It's not easy to go against the grain of what's popular with your friends. It takes strength and courage to tell these people that you don't want to get involved in something that's negative or wrong. But, if you really want to succeed, you'll have to step up and let go of negative people. Guys, these relationships aren't worth the price of your future.

- **Seek out and focus on positive relationships, and don't let anyone pull you away from them.** This applies to current and future relationships. And it involves boys, girls, and groups of people. Being connected with positive people who are doing positive things with their lives is a key to success. Look to school, church, and community organizations for these people.

- **Look for the signs, both positive and negative, that tell you about a person's true nature.** For example, a negative sign might be a girl who wants you to blow off your homework to come over to her house while her parents are gone. A positive sign might be a girl who says that you can't come over to her house while her parents aren't there. Also, be aware of "alarms." These should go off in any relationships that involve drugs, alcohol, gangs, crime, violence, and sex. These are the clear and loud alarms that tell you that a relationship is unhealthy for you.

Remember guys: The earlier that you can identify a relationship as a negative one, the easier it
is to get out of it. And, the chances of you getting involved in something unhealthy or negative are much less. So cut the person or group
of people loose at the first sign of trouble; don't
wait around to see if things might change.

- **Use your faith to handle pressures.** Pray and
  go to church; it will help you begin to understand that God always loves you and accepts
  you for who you are. A relationship with God
  through prayer and worship can give you
  positive feelings and the strength and courage
  needed to overcome negative and unhealthy
  relationships. Also, there are many positive
  people – both kids and adults – at church who
  are willing to help you learn more about how to
  build a relationship with God and how to solve
  relationship problems with others. But you can't
  get this help unless you show up, participate,
  and seek these people out.

- **Find positive people who are engaged in
  positive activities.** Where can you find these
  people? Lots of places! Here are some of them:
  school, sports clubs, church, YMCA, Boys and
  Girls Clubs, and many other community-based
  organizations. Most positive activities are organized, structured, and run by adults. That means

hanging out on the street corner with friends is not one of them! If you need help finding positive people, places, and activities in your community, ask a teacher or counselor at school. They'll be more than happy to help steer you in the right direction.

Guys, let's keep it real: Unhealthy relationships with individuals and groups of people carry all kinds of pressures, ones that usually lead to disastrous results. Ruining your future by doing whatever it takes to belong or fit in – no matter how dangerous, illegal, or wrong it is – isn't worth the price. Instead, look for positive people doing positive things, surround yourself with good friends, and draw positive energy from doing good things. Together, you can support and work with each other so that all succeed.

What Do You Think?

1. Why do some kids feel or give into the pressure to get involved in negative things?

_____

_____

_____

_____

_____

_____

_____

_____

_____

_____

_____

2. After reading this chapter, what can you do to resist the pressures around you?

_____

_____

_____

_____

_____

_____

_____

_____

_____

_____

_____

_____

_____

3. What are some of the bad pressures that you face in your own life today? How can you overcome them?

_____

_____

_____

_____

_____

_____

_____

_____

_____

_____

_____

_____

_____

_____

_____

4. What does Bill Cosby's quote at the beginning of the chapter say to you about how to handle pressure?

"Believe in life! Always human beings will live and progress to greater, broader, and fuller life."

W.E.B. DuBois
Writer and Teacher
(1868-1963)

The late 1800s was a difficult time in American history for African Americans. However, DuBois persevered in his studies and graduated from college in 1888. In 1895, he earned a Ph.D. from Harvard University. Later in life, DuBois helped found the National Association for the Advancement of Colored People (NAACP). He was also a recipient of the World Peace Council Prize. DuBois was a champion of African Americans and dedicated his life to equal rights. He was the most important African American protest leader in the United States during the first half of the 20th century.

Chapter 7

Faith and Spirituality

Guys, pay close attention to what's discussed in this chapter. It's about something that's really important to your life: your faith and spiritual life. I believe it's crucial for kids who want to reach their goals and dreams to have an active prayer and church life. Unfortunately, these things aren't part of some kids' lives. Why? Let's go over three reasons that I've heard from kids.

First, most kids have been told and taught that God is all-powerful, loving, and kind. It's hard for some kids who live in tough neighborhoods filled with poverty, crime, violence, drugs, and sex to understand how God can let things like this happen to them and those they love. Some kids expect God to "think and act" like they would. And when this doesn't happen, they are confused about how God and a strong faith and spiritual life can really help them.

Also, some kids tell me that they have "overdosed" on their faith and spirituality. They've had it forced on them so much since they were very young that, over time, prayer and going to church have become more like a chore. Rather than being positive experiences, faith and spirituality have become negative ones.

Finally, some kids say that faith or spiritual-based organizations aren't as fun, exciting, or stimulating compared to what's going on outside the church doors. Instead of being involved in learning more about God and their faith, some kids would rather be outside playing basketball or climbing on playground equipment with their friends.

I know you can come up with all sorts of reasons why you don't pray, go to church, or get involved in faith-based organizations and activities. But the bottom line still is that faith and spirituality play important roles in your success. Let's go over some reasons why all this is so important and ways to go about building a stronger faith and spiritual life:

- **Faith and spirituality are sources of hope and strength.** Everyone goes through difficult times during his or her life. Having a strong faith and relationship with God can give you the inspiration you need to keep moving forward.

- **You can make connections with positive people.** Getting involved in faith and spiritual-based organizations and activities leads you to people who are out to help others. And that includes you! They can help teach you about your faith and how to make it a positive part of your life. These people also can advise and guide you when you run into obstacles.

- **Faith and spirituality are all about positive messages.** And kids need to hear positive things! You need to hear that you're important and loved, and that your goals and dreams are worthy and attainable. One place you'll hear all these kinds of uplifting messages is through your faith.

- **When you participate in your faith, you'll find that you're accepted for who you are.** I know this because I found it to be true for me! This allows you to learn to become comfortable with who you are and how God made you. You don't experience the pressures to be someone different, like you often do with friends. It's comforting to go to a place and be with people who let you be yourself.

- **Your faith and the people involved in your faith can provide you with a lot of practical and intelligent information about how to live life and solve problems.** It's just a matter of you getting involved and seeking out help when you need it.

- **Prayer and church can give you a peaceful, positive place to go.** They can give you a much needed break from the turmoil and chaos that might be part of your life or environment. This allows you to refuel your spiritual tank so that you're able to persevere and keep on marching toward your goals.

- **Church and faith-based organizations offer fun and exciting things to do.** These places realize that kids need safe and positive places to go, and that kids learn differently from how adults learn. So they have developed activities that are specifically focused and designed for kids. Go check it out for yourself! There are lots of fun things for you to do: skits and plays; music, singing, and dancing; drawing and painting; field trips and outings; and much more!

- **Positive experiences can lead to more positive experiences.** They tend to build on themselves. It's kind of like a snowball rolling downhill that keeps getting bigger and bigger. The positive people and activities that you experience in your faith and at church can create the positive momentum you need to reach your goals and dreams.

Guys, let's keep it real: Faith and spirituality can play a very important role in your success. They provide you with positive people and inspiring messages. Prayer and church can be a source of strength during difficult times. So get involved! Learn how powerful these can be in your quest for success.

What Do You Think?

1. Why is your faith and having a relationship with God so important to your success?

_____

_____

_____

_____

_____

_____

_____

_____

_____

_____

_____

_____

_____

2. List and discuss the three reasons from the chapter why some kids do not develop a strong faith and spirituality in their lives.

3. How can you strengthen your faith and have a better relationship with God?

_____

_____

_____

_____

_____

_____

_____

_____

_____

_____

_____

_____

_____

4. What does W.E.B. DuBois's quote at the beginning of the chapter mean to you?

"The battles that count aren't the ones for gold medals. The struggles within yourself - the invisible, inevitable battles inside all of us - that's where it's at."

Jesse Owens
U.S. Track Star and
Olympic Gold Medal Winner
(1913 — 1980)

Jesse Owens was a gifted track and field athlete from an early age. While in high school, Owens won running and jumping events at national meets. In college, Owens set several world track and field records while competing for Ohio State University. At one meet, he equaled the world record for the 100-yard dash and broke the world records for the 220-yard dash, the 220-yard low hurdles, and the long jump. As a member of the United States team at the 1936 Olympic Games, Owens tied the Olympic record in the 100-meter run, broke Olympic and listed world records in the 200-meter run and the long jump, and ran the final leg for the world-record-breaking 4 x 100-meter relay team. His four Olympic victories were a blow to Adolf Hitler's intention to use the Olympic Games as a showcase of German superiority. For a time, Owens owned or shared world records for all sprint distances recognized by the International Amateur Athletic Federation. Owens' performance at the 1936 Olympics, combined with his efforts to help others after retiring from track and field, made him a revered African American figure.

Chapter 8

Self-Esteem

Self-esteem is something you've probably heard about but might not really understand. It's a concept that schools and other organizations and adults who work with and help kids say is important to success. I, too, believe this is true.

Some of you might have heard that self-esteem is how you "feel" about yourself. I don't believe that this is a good way to think about self-esteem. Why? Because feelings come and go. Your feelings can change by the hour, even by the minute. For example, someone might say something nice to you early in the day that makes you feel happy. Then, at lunch, someone might do something to you that's unkind, and suddenly you feel sad. When you base your self-esteem on how you feel at any given moment, you're allowing others and outside situations to determine how you perceive yourself as a person. You're also putting yourself at the mercy of what others might think, say, or do to you.

Who you are and your sense of worth should be developed and maintained from something more concrete than just feelings. So, what do I mean by "self-esteem"? Simply put, it's an accurate assessment of yourself. It means that you have a good and realistic understanding of your strengths and weaknesses and that you accept and are okay with them.

Sure, you have things to work on (we all do!), but the key to developing and maintaining healthy self-esteem is that you become comfortable with who you are and where you're headed. You know your strengths and you focus on them; you also know your weaknesses and are ready and willing to work on them. This kind of assessment helps you to develop a solid understanding of who you are and a belief in yourself that is not controlled by others and situations that you have no control over.

Let's discuss a bit more about self-esteem and some ways you can go about building and maintaining a strong sense of who you are and where you are headed.

- **Assess your strengths and weaknesses.** To know who you are and where you're headed, you've first got to identify the things you do well and what you need to get better at. Do this by writing down your strengths and weaknesses. Ask a trusted, caring adult who knows you well to guide you in this process. An objective, outside view from another person will help you arrive at the most accurate assessment possible.

- **Focus on improvement.** We all know it's important to pay attention to and improve on areas that need improvement. This helps us to become better people and enables us to have a better chance at success. But don't forget about improving your strengths! These are usually the things that help you to fully understand who you are and where you're headed. For example, if you enjoy and are good in school, challenge yourself by taking more advanced classes or by getting involved in extracurricular academic activities. Just because something is already a strength doesn't mean you can't get better at it!

- **Ask for help.** I know it was very beneficial for me to ask for help when I was getting to know who I was and where I was headed. Your knowledge and perspective is limited to what you know and what you have experienced up to this point in your life. Others can bring a knowledge base and perspective that's new, fresh, and filled with experience. They can point out strengths and weaknesses that you can't see, aren't aware of, or never would have considered. So seek out a parent, teacher, school counselor, coach, or other caring, trusted adult who knows you well.

- **Be careful not to let others decide for you who you are and where you're headed.** There's a big difference between asking for guidance and letting someone take control. Ultimately, you've got to be the one who makes the decisions. Why? If what you want to do with your life is someone else's idea, then you may not be totally committed to seeing things through. It's more likely that you might give up or quit when the going gets tough. When it's your decision, you take ownership and you're more likely to do whatever it takes to succeed – no matter the obstacles!

- **Relationships don't define you.** Sure, your relationships with your family and friends are important. And they play an important role in forming who you are and where you're headed. But, they don't have the last and only say in all this. Some of you might come from families that are pretty messed up. But that doesn't mean you can't succeed! Your planning, effort, and focus are what matters – not your family history or situation.

- **Remain positive in the face of negativity.** Sometimes people say and do things to you that will make you angry or sad. People might even tell you that you're not worth much and that who you are and where you're headed is stupid and wrong. Guys, don't listen to this stuff! Remain upbeat and positive when you hear such talk, then turn around and stay away from these people. Don't let their negative words or actions sway you from your march to success! Instead, seek out positive people and activities that support your goals and dreams.

- **Stay humble.** I'll bet you've seen others (adults and kids) treat kids who are sports stars differently from kids who aren't as athletically gifted. The same might happen with kids who are gifted in school, art, or music. But how many times have you seen those kids change and become selfish and self-centered? Too much or the wrong kind of attention can do this to kids. If people say good things about you and treat you well, don't let it go to your head. Always remain grateful, gracious, and humble.

- **It's okay to have problems.** Everyone struggles and faces obstacles – these things are part of life. And you're going to make mistakes and fail. But guys, this is when learning and growth happen. Don't put pressure on yourself to be perfect. Cut yourself some slack when problems crop up. Forge ahead and do the best you can to work through them. You'll be stronger because of it!

- **Serve and help others.** It's important for you to get out of yourself and put others first. A natural outcome of doing this is feeling good about who you are and where you're headed. So go help a neighbor with yard work or spend some time talking with an elderly person who might be lonely. There are hundreds of things you can do in your community, school, and church to lend a helping hand and make a positive difference!

- **Live a healthy lifestyle.** Take care of yourself physically, mentally, and spiritually. Live an organized and disciplined life. This means eating right, getting enough sleep, exercising, studying, playing, relaxing, talking to others when things are bothering you, praying, etc. All this will help you build and maintain a positive sense of who you are and where you're headed.

- **Take care of business.** You have certain obligations at home, school, and church. For example, you might have chores at home and homework for school. Make sure that you get these kinds of things done before you go out and spend time with your friends. Doing this over and over leads to developing the good habit of taking responsibility. And once this becomes a habit, you've got another tool for success.

- **Participate in your faith.** As you grow and become active in your faith, you come to learn that God accepts you for exactly who you are. You come to feel and know that God will always love you. This is a great comfort when times get tough!

Guys, let's keep it real: Take the time to assess your strengths and weaknesses. Doing this gives you a concrete and accurate way of uncovering who you are and what you want in life. Once you identify and are confident in these things, you are on your way to success!

What Do You Think?

1. Why is self-esteem more than just feeling good about yourself?

_____

_____

_____

_____

_____

_____

_____

_____

_____

_____

_____

_____

_____

2. What can you do to develop a more positive
   outlook about yourself and your life?

3. Why is assessing your strengths and weaknesses important to your success? What are your strengths? What are your weaknesses?

_____

_____

_____

_____

_____

_____

_____

_____

_____

_____

_____

_____

_____

4. How can you apply Jesse Owens' quote at the beginning of the chapter to your own life?

"When you clench your fist, no one can put anything in your hand, nor can your hand pick up anything."

Alex Haley
Author
(1921 – 1992)

Although his parents were teachers, Haley was a mediocre student. He began writing to avoid boredom during voyages while serving in the U.S. Coast Guard. His first major work, *The Autobiography of Malcolm X*, was a widely read book based on Haley's interviews with the Black Muslim leader. The work is recognized as a classic of black American autobiography. Haley's greatest success as an author was for his book *Roots: The Saga of an American Family*. The idea and content for the book came from the oral family history told to him by his grandmother. The story covers seven American generations, from the enslavement of Haley's African ancestors to his own quest to trace his family tree. *Roots* was adapted as a multi-episode television program, which, when first broadcast in January 1977, became one of the most popular shows in the history of American television. That same year, Haley won a special Pulitzer Prize.

Chapter 9

Loneliness

Many teenagers experience loneliness. Loneliness is not the same as being alone. Sometimes, you can feel lonely even when you're surrounded by family or other people.

It's natural for kids your age to go through periods of loneliness. For most, these periods are usually short and quickly resolved. But there are a number of kids, especially African American teenage boys, who experience a kind of loneliness that overtakes and dominates their lives. It can be a crippling feeling. These kids feel despair, sadness, and hopelessness because they don't believe there is anyone they can go to for love and guidance.

There are a couple of reasons for this. First, many African American teenage boys are being reared in single-parent homes by their mothers. In many homes, this means that moms are working two and three jobs just to make ends meet. It also means that there are a lot of mothers who don't have the kind of time they would like to spend with their kids. As a result, kids can feel lonely because there simply isn't a parent around to talk to and spend quality time with.

I believe that the biggest reason African American teenage boys feel lonely is because many grow up without a father who is active in their lives. This can be a devastating experience. Not having a relationship with a father creates a tremendous void in a boy's life.

Without the stability a father can bring to a family, most boys look to other people and places to fill the psychological, emotional, and physical void. When there's no positive male adult support or guidance, many teenage boys turn to gangs, alcohol, drugs, or sex as a way to relieve their loneliness.

Guys, let's keep it real: There are some pretty nasty people out there who prey on kids who are lonely and looking for some kind – any kind – of relationship or connection. Gang leaders and drug dealers are always hunting for kids who just want to feel like they're part of something. These bad guys will try to create a false sense of relationship and connection with you as a way to recruit and use you for dangerous criminal activity. So don't be fooled. These gang leaders and drug dealers do not care about you; they just want to use you to help them make money in illegal and dangerous ways. Remember, these people are using the void that an absent father can create as a way to pull you in.

Okay, now that we know what loneliness is, what can cause it, and the dangers it can lead to, let's go over some ways you can avoid or overcome loneliness in your life.

- **Develop and maintain positive relationships.** This applies to your relationships with family, friends, and others. Loneliness often results from relationships that have been damaged in some way. Usually, relationships fall apart because they haven't been properly developed or maintained. It's like a plant that doesn't get watered. Eventually, the plant withers and dies. The same thing can happen with any of your relationships. It takes two people to build a good, positive relationship. So make sure that you keep your side of the street clean by doing the right things to help your relationships grow and prosper in a healthy way.

- **Don't be exclusive in your relationships, especially with girls!** Many times, boys and girls get into relationships where they don't allow each other to have friendships with other boys and girls. When this happens, you think that a girl is "yours" and that she can't even talk to other guys. I know you've heard this before, but I've got to say it again: You should have lots of friends, both girls and guys. It's a fun and healthy way to travel through your teenage years. When you get locked up into a relationship with only one girl, you're setting yourself up for loneliness. How? It's very unusual for two teens to have an exclusive relationship, stay together for years and eventually get married. Most teenage boy-girl relationships don't last very long – for many different reasons. If you allow yourself to become so emotionally invested in only one relationship, then you're setting yourself up for disappointment, heartache, and loneliness. So, spread yourself around and enjoy getting to know many different people.

- **Get involved in groups that are doing positive things.** This is a great way to meet and get to know many different people. Positive groups help you to fill the void created by loneliness without experiencing the problems that come with an exclusive relationship. In a group, you can build many relationships. If one friendship that you have in the group breaks down or simply fades a bit, you still have other relationships within the group. So get involved in school, community, and church groups that are doing positive things. It's not only fun but it'll rid your life of loneliness.

- **Don't get trapped by a bad environment.** Many kids who come from poor and rough neighborhoods feel isolated. It may be dangerous for them to even go outside. This can make kids feel like they're physically trapped inside their own home, which can lead to feelings of loneliness. This is why it's important for you to get involved in extracurricular activities before or after school or to volunteer to be part of faith-based and community activities. People who care about kids' safety lead these activities, and they're usually held in places where you can feel safe. Being involved and interacting with others is the best cure for loneliness.

- **Help out at home.** When a family is struggling financially, it can lead to frustration and strained relationships between parent and child. This happened to me with my father. He worked 12 hours a day just to keep a roof over our head and food on our table. Because he worked so hard, he wasn't around a lot for me to talk to, and when he was at home, he was tired from a long day's work. He just couldn't give the time and energy we would have liked to have had when we were together. That's why it's important for you to help out at home. When you contribute by doing chores and making sure your homework's done, it's one less thing that your mother or father has to worry about. And this frees up more time for him or her to spend with you.

- **Look to your family.** There are positive role models in almost every extended family whom you can go to for guidance and support. Some kids might have to look harder and longer to find these people. But once you find them it's like finding gold! This person might be an older bother, sister, grandparent, uncle, or aunt. Growing up, my older brother was an extremely positive influence for me when it came to school. He encouraged and helped me to be the best student possible. When I needed someone to talk to and get advice from, he was always glad to help. There are probably people in your family who are just like that. Look at the people who are doing positive things in their lives and seek them out. Ask them to be part of your journey to success. If you sincerely want their help, they'll be glad to give it to you!

- **Look to your faith.** Continue to develop a positive relationship with God. This is the one relationship where all the action is up to you. By going to church and praying, you have the opportunity to experience a relationship where you're always loved and accepted. Guys, trust me on this one: When your relationship with God is right, you will never feel all alone!

- **Get up and get out.** Don't wait for positive people and activities to come to you. It doesn't work like that. You've got to do the footwork. At school, go ask a teacher or coach how you can get involved. Do the same thing in your community and church. Sitting at home doing nothing just invites loneliness. Being involved can go a long way toward relieving these feelings.

- **Talk to others.** When you're feeling lonely, talk about it with positive people in your life – a parent, relative, teacher, counselor, or coach. Reach out and tell someone who cares about you. Most times, just getting these feelings off your chest makes you feel better right away. Bottling it up inside only increases and intensifies your negative thoughts and feelings. Also, you can express your feelings by drawing or writing in a journal.

- **Take action.** Many times when you're feeling bad or lonely, all you want to do is sit around and do nothing. Guys, that's the last thing to do! When this happens, even though you might not want to, force yourself to take a positive action. There are lots of things you can do to get yourself out of a funk: go exercise, help a neighbor with a chore, visit an elderly person who might be lonely, or volunteer to help with an activity at church or community center. Your list of positive actions can be as long as you want it to be! The important thing to remember is don't sit around feeling sorry for yourself; instead, force yourself to take a positive action. When you do, you'll feel better pretty quickly!

Guys, let's keep it real: Loneliness comes from relationships in your life that have been damaged or broken in some way or from not having healthy relationships at all. If you're not careful, loneliness can consume you and lead you into a world of negative people and activities and trouble. Stay strong by seeking out positive people who are doing positive things. That's where you'll find the healthy relationships you're looking for that will help you on your journey to success.

What Do You Think?

1. What are two ways that lead to kids feeling lonely? How do they apply to your life?

2. What are the dangers of letting loneliness take over your thoughts and actions?

3. What are some ways to overcome loneliness? How can you put them to work in your life?

4. Ask a relative or a friend what he or she thinks Alex Haley's quote at the beginning of the chapter means. Write the response here. Do you agree?

"Pleasure is not happiness. It has no more importance than a shadow following a man."

————————————————

Muhammad Ali
Professional Boxer
and Social Activist
(Born 1942)

Ali grew up in the American South during a time of segregated public facilities. His father painted billboards and signs and his mother was a maid. When Ali was 12, he took up boxing. Through hard work and dedication, Ali advanced through the amateur ranks. In 1960, he won a gold medal in the Olympics and then began a professional boxing career. Ali was the first fighter to win the world heavyweight championship on three separate occasions, and he successfully defended this title 19 times. During the prime of his boxing career, Ali refused to participate in the Vietnam War because of his religious beliefs. He was jailed and banned from boxing for years, but never wavered from his beliefs. Ali's example of strength in his convictions continues to be a source of inspiration for many Americans.

Chapter 10

Pain and Pleasure

Success and reaching goals come with a price. That price may be big or small. It all depends on the goal and how bad you want it.

I'm going to get right to the point. This chapter is all about one concept: sacrifice. What do I mean here? It's really very simple: If you want to be successful and reach your goals, you have to give up some things you enjoy doing and do some things you don't like doing.

Guys, you can't have it all, especially *all* of the time. For example, if your goal is to go to college, you're going to have to spend less time hanging out with your homeboys and more time doing homework and studying. This is the price you must pay. You will have to sacrifice doing only what you enjoy to do tough, hard things to reach your goals.

Sacrifice is a difficult thing for many kids your age. I know it was for me. I enjoyed being around my friends, but over time, I realized that if I wanted to make progress toward my goals I needed to commit to doing whatever it took to reach them. And for me, that meant spending more time doing the big and little things – whether I liked doing them or not – needed for success.

What are those big and little things? Let's go over some of them. The following lessons are ones I've learned from others and in my own experiences with sacrifice and what it means to reaching goals:

- **Learn to say "No."** This is probably the most important thing I've learned when it comes to sacrifice. There will always be someone who has a tempting offer or who will try to talk you out of taking care of your responsibilities. It may be a friend who wants you to play video games or a girl who wants to spend lots of time talking on the phone with you. Guys, if you want to reach your goals and succeed, you have to learn to tell these people "No," especially when you have to take care of things like homework, chores, or other responsibilities. Be proud of what you're trying to accomplish and don't let others interfere with your goals. Just tell them, "No thank you." Now, does this mean you can never have fun? Of course not! It simply means that you have to take care of business first. After all your responsibilities are done, then it's time to do what you enjoy.

- **Make a road map to success.** Put your goals down on paper. Write out exactly what you want to do and how you intend to go about accomplishing it. Then, prioritize what comes first, second, third, and so on. If you need help doing this, don't hesitate to ask a trusted, caring adult for assistance. Once all this is done, then comes the hard part: sticking to it! There will probably be times when you stray from your plan. But since you've got it all organized and written down, it's less likely to happen as often, and when you do stray, it'll be easier to get back on track. It may take some time to put together a good, thorough plan, but trust me on this one, it'll be worth it! A road map will give you confidence and direction, two important ingredients for success.

- **Stop and think.** Lots of times, kids allow themselves to be guided by their emotions and feelings. This can lead to the mindset that "if it feels good, do it." Unfortunately, a few moments of pleasure can lead to a lifetime of pain and heartache. This is very true when it comes to sex, drugs, alcohol, gangs, and violence. When you allow your life to be driven by emotions and a desire for pleasure, you are bound to make poor choices and decisions. That's why it's important to stop and think before you act. Ask yourself if the next action you're going to take will get you closer to your goals or farther away. If you're honest, the answer will be crystal clear.

- **Be patient.** Learning to wait for certain things is hard for kids today. There's pressure from others to do and have certain things. The pressure seems to be greatest when it comes to sex and money. Many kids tell me that they feel pressure to have sex at an early age and to own certain expensive items (shoes, clothes, cell phones, jewelry, etc.). These things might look attractive but they can't be your sole focus. Guys, you've got all your life to experience these things. Be patient; wait until you're older and wiser. Good things do come to those who wait. Allow life to unfold at its own pace; don't force it. You job is to be patient and to make good decisions for the long run.

- **Find positive hobbies.** Read, draw, write, sing, play a musical instrument, get involved in a club, go out for a play, play a sport, etc. All these are healthy, fun, and exciting ways to spend your time. And they can keep you away from the negative temptations, people, and activities that might be around you. Guys, there are many positive things to do and get involved in at school, in your community, and at church. But you have to make the move to go find them. So, just do it!

- **Be courageous!** It's not easy to sacrifice and to tell your friends "No." You run the risk of being made fun of or not being included. In order to succeed, though, there will be times when you have to stand alone. Be the kind of brave person who sets his own stage; don't allow others to set it for you. Remain strong in your convictions and focused on your goals. Stand up for what's right and good for you and others.

- **Look to history.** There are many great role models in African American history who have proved that sacrifice can lead to success. Look to their example and stories for strength and inspiration, and use their experiences as a guide for your own life. Many of these people had lives filled with tremendous obstacles, but they found a way, through persistence and hard work, to reach their goals and dreams. You can do the very same thing! You can find books about these people's lives in the school or city library. Go check them out and read, read, read!

- **Be realistic.** There are certain things you can have and do right now. Don't get ahead of yourself. At your age, it's important to spend the majority of your time at school and doing schoolwork. Cars, stereos, jewelry, clothes and other things that cost lots of money to get and maintain shouldn't be a priority right now for your long-term success. So don't focus on accumulating these kinds of things. Stay realistic about where you are in life and what's important for you to do today so that you can succeed tomorrow.

- **Don't take shortcuts.** Guys, this one's pretty simple but it's very important. Your goals can be reached only through hard work and determination. Avoid the temptation to take shortcuts. They will only lead you off your path to success and make the journey longer and harder. Remember that success requires effort. Be prepared and willing to do the work it takes to reach your goals. It's all worth it in the end!

Guys, let's keep it real: It takes courage to tell a friend you can't do something fun because of school or home responsibilities or to go to a job that you don't particularly like, but need. But, by sacrificing and doing the tough things today, you're setting yourself up for success tomorrow. Sacrifice teaches you discipline, self-control and, confidence. All these are important skills for realizing your goals and dreams.

What Do You Think?

1. After reading this chapter, what does "sacrifice" mean to you?

_____

_____

_____

_____

_____

_____

_____

_____

_____

_____

_____

_____

_____

2. Why should you sometimes say "No" to friends?

_____

_____

_____

_____

_____

_____

_____

_____

_____

_____

_____

_____

_____

_____

3. Why are going to school and getting an education important to success? What can you do to
   make them top priorities in your life?

_____

_____

_____

_____

_____

_____

_____

_____

_____

_____

_____

_____

4. Ask a teacher to read Muhammad Ali's quote at the beginning of the chapter and tell you what it means to him or her. Write the response here.

_____

_____

_____

_____

_____

_____

_____

_____

_____

_____

_____

_____

_____

"None of us got where we are solely by pulling ourselves up by our bootstraps. We got here because somebody - a parent, a teacher, an Ivy League crony or a few nuns - bent down and helped us pick up our boots."

Thurgood Marshall
Supreme Court Justice
(1908 –1993)

After college, Thurgood Marshall went to law school, where he graduated first in his class. Marshall then went to work for the National Association for the Advancement of Colored People (NAACP), and eventually became chief of its legal staff. During that time, he won 29 of the 32 cases that he argued before the U.S. Supreme Court. He successfully argued many landmark cases that involved racial injustices, including Brown vs. Board of Education of Topeka. Years later, President Lyndon B. Johnson appointed Marshall to the Supreme Court. He was the first African American to sit on the high court. While there, he consistently supported positions taken by those challenging discrimination based on race or sex.

Chapter 11

Role Models

Millions of kids have seen and heard the advertising slogan "Be like Mike" on TV. But what is this phrase telling you? Simply put, it's saying that if you want to be like Michael Jordan, all you have to do is buy what he's selling. It's an advertising ploy intended to influence you to purchase the products that Michael Jordan endorses.

Directing this kind of advertising at kids bothers me for a few reasons. I'm not going to get into all of them here. I just want to talk about the one reason that's relevant to this chapter on role models.

From what I've heard and seen from kids today, they've taken the phrase, "Be like Mike," a step further. Not only do kids want the products Michael Jordan is pitching, but they also want to be like Mike in every way possible. That means they want to be an NBA basketball player, complete with all the fame and fortune.

Today, many kids look to famous athletes, singers, musicians, actors, and other celebrities as role models – or people they admire, respect, and want to be like. But celebrities are not always people you should look to as role models. Let's talk about a couple of reasons why I believe this to be true.

- **These people are untouchable, meaning they simply are not available to you.** Real role models are people who are there for you every day to help guide you through life's ups and downs. Let's keep it real: You can't call up or visit famous athletes, singers, and musicians whenever a difficult problem or situation arises. These people may be wonderful entertainers, but they aren't role models because they aren't and can't be a part of your everyday life.

- **Idolizing professional athletes and celebrities can lead you to overlook people who *can* be real role models for you.** You could undervalue and even dismiss the lives of possible role models like your father, uncle, teacher, or coach because they don't have the kind of fame or material success a celebrity or professional athlete has. Guys, this kind of comparison is unfair and it often leads to disrespectful, strained, or broken relationships with the people who are most important in your life and to your success.

Okay, I think you get the point that professional athletes, musicians, and singers don't always make the best role models. So, who does? When I work with and teach kids about this very subject, I advise them to look for their "everyday heroes." These people can be found in your home, school, neighborhood, and community. They can be family members, relatives, neighbors, teachers, coaches, barbers, mechanics, plumbers – anyone!

Everyday heroes may be different in many ways, but they all possess a majority, if not all, of the following qualities. These qualities are what make them good role models:

- They've persevered and risen above adversity. After all, there's no one better to teach you all about getting back up when you've been knocked down than someone who's done it himself or herself.

- They are positive, upbeat, and optimistic.

- They are determined, work hard, and aren't afraid to tackle tough problems.

- They are kind, helpful, and generous.

- They are unselfish and willing to put others first.

- They are encouraging and honest.

- They're humble and give credit to others when it's due.

- They look for positive solutions to problems.

As you can see, nowhere does it say that a good role model has to be able to dunk a basketball or pound out a great rap song. Everyday heroes are all around you. All you have to do is take your focus off the professional athletes and celebrities and open your eyes! An everyday hero might be a neighbor who spends his free time helping to repair an elderly neighbor's car. Or it might be a relative who volunteers to coach your team at the local community center. An everyday hero certainly is a father who lives at home, takes care of his wife and kids, works a full day, and goes to church on Sunday.

You see, fellas, most of these people are right under your noses. You just haven't been looking in the right places. Everyday heroes probably don't have fancy cars and expensive stuff, but they have what it takes to help guide you on your journey to success.

Don't discount the importance of having an "everyday hero" in your life. He or she can be instrumental in helping you to achieve your goals and dreams. Here are some ways they can do this:

- They encourage and inspire you to keep striving despite obstacles.

- They are sources of knowledge, experience, and wisdom.

- They always help you keep hope alive.

- They help you come to positive solutions to problems.

- They are real-life examples of how you can succeed.

- They are sounding boards when you want to talk about your thoughts and feelings – both good and bad – and about your hopes and dreams.

- They teach you positive life lessons and skills needed for success.

Guys, let's keep it real: When it comes to looking for role models, keep your focus on the everyday heroes around you. In your life, professional athletes, singers, musicians, and other celebrities are simply entertainers, not role models. They're not people who can be active in helping you solve and overcome day-to-day problems and obstacles. But everyday heroes can! These are the people who really love and care about you and your future.

What Do You Think?

1. Why do most famous athletes, singers, musicians, actors, and other celebrities make poor role models for kids?

2. Explain what an everyday hero means to you.

_____

_____

_____

_____

_____

_____

_____

_____

_____

_____

_____

_____

_____

_____

_____

3. What positive qualities do everyday heroes possess?

4. Who are some of your role models? Why are
   they good role models for you?

_____

_____

_____

_____

_____

_____

_____

_____

_____

_____

_____

_____

_____

_____

_____

"A sure way for one to
lift himself up is by
helping to lift someone
else."

───────────────

Booker T. Washington
American Educator and Reformer
(1856 – 1915)

Born a slave and deprived of any early education,
Booker Taliaferro Washington went on to become
America's foremost African American educator of
the early 20th century. He was the first principal
at the Tuskegee Institute, where he championed
vocational training as a means for African American
self-reliance. A well-known orator, Washington
also wrote a best-selling autobiography and advised
Presidents Theodore Roosevelt and William Taft on
race relations.

Chapter 12

Purpose

Guys, each one of you is different in many ways. When it comes to purpose, however, I believe that you are all very similar. Let me explain.

God gives each one of you different gifts – or talents. These gifts are things that you are good at and enjoy doing, and they have a positive influence and effect on you and others. Gifts are wide and varied and can include talents like drawing, writing, singing, speaking, listening, and many others. Some of you might have gifts that help you do well in school, sports, music, and other areas in life.

Your job – or purpose – is to make sure that you use your gifts in ways that benefit others and the world around you. I believe this is the ultimate purpose for every human being. To put it even more simply, purpose can be boiled down to the Golden Rule: Treat others only in ways that you want to be treated. This purpose is what makes you all similar. What's different is how each one of you goes about using your individual gifts to accomplish this purpose.

Now, no one is perfect. Sometimes in life you can lose your way and allow your thoughts and actions to drift away from your true purpose. Let's talk about two ways this can happen:

- **Your gifts are not your purpose.** But many kids define themselves by their gifts. This means, for example, that some kids believe that what they do and accomplish in school, sports, on the job, or in other areas of life determines who they are as a person. And they believe that their purpose is to achieve as much as they can no matter the costs to themselves and others. When this happens, your real purpose strays from focusing on how to use your gifts to benefit others and the world around you, and it shines directly and only on you and your accomplishments. It becomes all about achievements, while helping others is put on the back burner. Guys, this is just wrong thinking.

- **Some kids use their gifts as a way to get what they want.** For example, I've seen some kids get lots of praise and pats on the back because they are gifted in sports. Some of these kids turn around and use this gift to get what they want from others, whether it's getting breaks on grades in school from their teachers or getting things for free (money, clothes, etc.) from others. When kids do this, they are being selfish because they are using their gifts only to benefit themselves.

Remember, your gifts were given to you by God. He gave them to you so you would have ways to serve others and the world around you. The challenge for you each and every day is to remember this and to use your gifts in the right ways.

So, what can you do to better understand and accept your gifts and to use them positively? Here are some suggestions I've learned from others and from my own journey:

- **Remember what your purpose is and what it is not.** Your purpose is not about what you do in a job or what you accomplish in school, sports, or at work. It's not about how much money you make or the expensive things you own. Achieving goals and owning things are fine, as long as you stay humble and keep your eye on the real meaning of life. That means that no matter what you accumulate or what you accomplish, you still understand that it all comes back to the Golden Rule.

- **Recognize and uncover your gifts.** You have to know what your gifts are in order to use them. For some of you, your gifts will be obvious and easy to see. For others, however, it may be harder for you to see your gifts. For example, you might be a great listener but you don't recognize this as a gift. So, if you're unsure about what your gifts are, go to a caring, loving adult and ask him or her for help. Sometimes, others easily see what we are unable to see in ourselves. Once you uncover and recognize your gifts, start using them in positive ways!

- **Talk to your role models.** These are people who love and care about you. Share your thoughts and feeling with them about your gifts. Ask them for ways you can use your gifts to help others and the world around you. They'll help you come up with positive and constructive ways to put your gifts to good use.

- **Go to church.** This is a place where you can gain knowledge of and learn many lessons about gifts and purpose. At church, there are pastors or priests who have experience in and are specially trained to help people learn about their gifts and purpose. At many churches, there are even activities designed to help kids with these very issues. So go check it out! Participate in your church and discover all of the wonderful spiritual guidance that is offered there.

- **Pray daily.** Ask God through prayer for help
  and guidance with your gifts and talents. He'll
  help you come to understand your gifts better
  and how to use them in positive ways. If you
  want to learn more about prayer or how to pray,
  talk to adults, especially those at your church
  (priests or pastors too!) who make prayer part
  of their daily life. Guys, prayer can be a powerful part of your life. I know it was for me at your
  age and it continues to be today!

- **Take action and get involved!** This one sounds
  pretty simple and it is. Many times, kids just
  don't know where to put their gifts to good use.
  But there are lots of places: school, church, faith-
  based organizations, community-based organizations, Girls and Boys Clubs, the YMCA, and
  many others. Simply take the time and action to
  get involved in the positive activities that go on
  in these places. They need you and your gifts to
  make a difference in others' lives.

Guys, let's keep it real: When you learn, understand, and use your gifts for the purpose of helping others and the world around you, you have
achieved true success. Remember, success is not
measured in dollars and cents, athletic ability,
college degrees, money, jobs, cars, homes, or the
accumulation of accomplishments and "things."
True success is measured by the positive impact

and influence you have on others and the world. So step up! Use those wonderful gifts you've been given to make a positive difference in your family, the community, and the world.

What Do You Think?

1. What are some of your gifts and talents? How have you put these to positive use in your life?

_____

_____

_____

_____

_____

_____

_____

_____

_____

_____

_____

_____

_____

_____

2. What is your *ultimate* purpose? How can you go about achieving this?

_____

_____

_____

_____

_____

_____

_____

_____

_____

_____

_____

_____

_____

_____

_____

_____

3. What are two ways you can drift from your
   true purpose?

4. Ask a parent or older relative (grandparent, aunt, uncle, etc.) to read Booker T. Washington's quote at the beginning of the chapter and tell you what it means to him or her. Write the response here. What do you think it means?

_____

_____

_____

_____

_____

_____

_____

_____

_____

_____